By Laura Williams
Translated by Emi Takahashi

© 2022 Williams Books
1 rue de l'église, 91430 Igny
Dépôt légal : Décembre 2022
ISBN 978-2-494614-39-0
Imprimé à la demande par Amazon
Loi n° 49-956 du 16 juillet 1949 sur les publications destinées à la jeunesse

りんご

[ringo] – apple

アボカド
[abokado] – avocado

バナナ
[banana] - banana

豆

[mame] - beans

キャベツ

[kyabetsu] – cabbage

にんじん
[ninjin] – carrot

チリ
[chiri] – chilli

とうもろこし
[toumorokoshi] – corn

キュウリ

[kyuuri] – cucumber

ナス

[nasu] – eggplant

ニンニク
[ninniku] - garlic

生姜
[shouga] – ginger

インゲン

[ingen] – green beans

グアバ
[guaba] – guava

レモン
[remon] - lemon

マンゴー
[mango] - *mango*

キノコ

[kinoko] – mushroom

玉ねぎ

[tamanegi] – onion

オレンジ

[orenji] – orange

パパイヤ

[papaiya] – papaya

パッションフルーツ
[passhonfurutsu] - passion fruit

ピーナッツ

[pinattsu] - peanut

グリーンピース
[gurinpisu] - peas

パイナップル
[painappuru] – pineapple

ポテト

[poteto] - potato

カボチャ
[kabocha] - pumpkin

米 [kome] – rice

大豆
[daizu] − soy

ほうれん草
[hourensou] - spinach

サトウキビ
[satoukibi] - sugar cane

サツマイモ

[satsumaimo] – sweet potato

トマト

[tomato] – tomato

スイカ

[suika] - watermelon

小麦 [komugi] – wheat

Thank you

Thank you for purchasing "Japanese-English Words for Toddlers"! Your support means a lot to me, and I hope you and your child enjoy these books.

If you have a moment, I would greatly appreciate it if you could leave a review on Amazon. Your feedback will help me improve future editions of the series and create more resources for bilingual children.

Thank you again for your support. You can access the reviews on Amazon by scanning the QR code below or by visiting the link below:

https://www.amazon.com/review/create-review?&asin=2494614392

Thank you for helping me continue my work as a language teacher and translator. Your support is greatly appreciated!

In the same collection

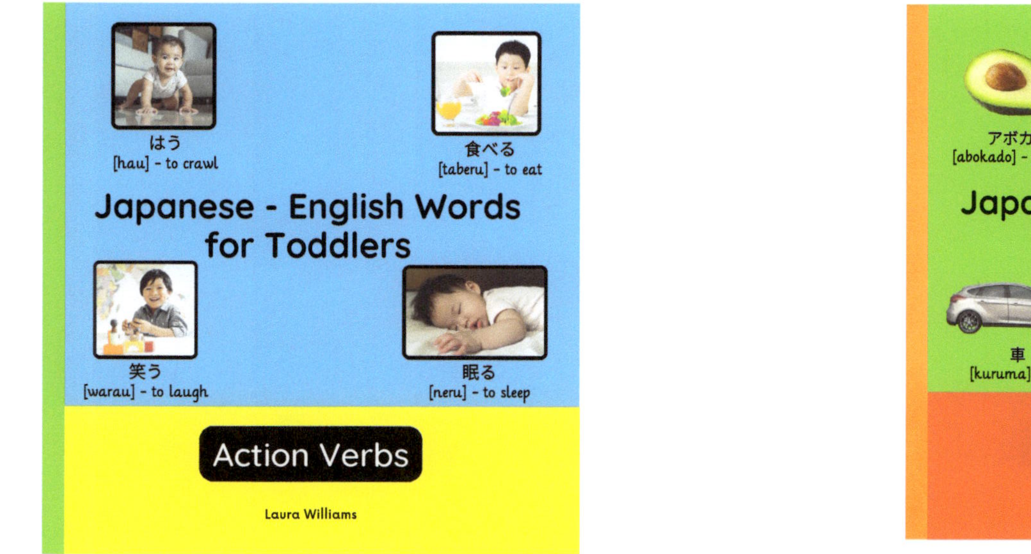

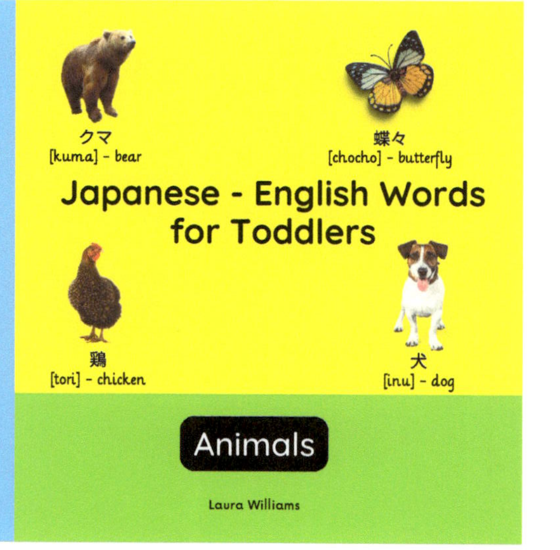